pumpkins & squashes

pumpkins & squashes

Transform your menu and create inspirational
meals with the most versatile of vegetables

Love Food ® is an imprint of Parragon Books Ltd

Parragon
Queen Street House
4 Queen Street
Bath BA1 1HE, UK

ISBN: 978-1-4075-3385-8

Printed in China

Introduction and recipes written by Anne Sheasby
Photography by Clive Streeter
Food styling by Angela Drake and Teresa Goldfinch
Internal design by Shelley Doyle

Notes for the Reader

This book uses imperial, metric, and U.S. cup measurements. Follow the same units of measurement throughout; do not mix imperial and metric. All spoon measurements are level: teaspoons are assumed to be 5 ml, and tablespoons are assumed to be 15 ml. Unless otherwise stated, milk is assumed to be whole, eggs and individual vegetables, such as potatoes, are medium, and pepper is freshly ground black pepper.

The times given are an approximate guide only. Preparation times differ according to the techniques used by different people and the cooking times may also vary from those given as a result of the type of oven used. Optional ingredients, variations, or serving suggestions have not been included in the calculations.

Recipes using raw or very lightly cooked eggs should be avoided by infants, the elderly, pregnant women, convalescents, and anyone with a chronic condition. Pregnant and breastfeeding women are advised to avoid eating peanuts and peanut products. People with nut allergies should be aware that some of the prepared ingredients used in the recipes in this book may contain nuts. Always check the packaging before use.

contents

TYPES OF PUMPKINS AND SQUASHES

Pumpkins and squashes are a popular and versatile group of vegetables that are widely used in cooking to create a wonderful array of exciting and tempting recipes, both savory and sweet.

There are many varieties of pumpkins and squashes, the majority of which are edible, with a few that tend to be used for only decoration. Pumpkins, squashes, zucchini, cucumbers, gherkins, gourds, and melons are all members of the cucumber family (cucurbitaceae) and they come in a wide range of shapes, sizes, and colors.

There are two main types of squash—summer squash and winter squash—but this can be a slightly misleading division, because many varieties are now readily available all year round. Summer squashes are at their best from around midsummer to mid-fall, and winter squashes are in their prime from around late summer to mid or late fall, depending on the variety. In this book we are concentrating on the most popular summer and winter squashes, including zucchini, butternut squash, and pumpkins.

Within the two subgroups of summer and winter squashes, many recipes are interchangeable, so, for example, if a recipe calls for a winter squash, such as butternut squash, but you only have an alternative winter squash, such as acorn squash or pumpkin at hand, then the chances are that the recipe will work just as well with any of the winter squash options. The same applies to summer squashes, although the variety and alternatives are more limited.

OTHER VARIETIES OF PUMPKINS & SQUASHES

Varieties of squashes and pumpkins vary around the world and are too numerous to mention in detail, but we do include information on other types of popular squashes, such as acorn squash, buttercup squash, delicata squash, hubbard squash, kabocha squash, and spaghetti squash. Also, this book would not be complete without a quick mention of the wonderful exotic names of some of the lesser-known squashes, such as Iran winter squash, red etampes squash, red kuri squash, and Ukranian winter squash.

SUMMER SQUASHES

Generally speaking, summer squashes, such as zucchini, are quick-growing and relatively small in size, with thin skins, soft edible seeds, and a pale, soft, watery flesh that has a delicate flavor. When eaten young, summer squashes usually require no peeling and they cook quickly. Young zucchini are also edible raw and can be grated, thinly sliced, or shaved into ribbons to create the basis for a refreshing summer salad.

There are many types of summer squashes available, in varying shades of green and yellow, and in varying shapes, including the classic cucumber-like zucchini and the disk-shaped pattypan squash. Some zucchini are even the shape and size of a tennis ball.

Summer squashes, such as zucchini, naturally go well with plenty of other flavors and ingredients, including tomatoes, bell peppers, onions, eggplant, garlic, chiles, herbs, such as basil, oregano, or mint, olive oil, butter, cheese, such as Parmesan, eggs, cream, ginger, and lemon.

Key Nutrients

Summer squashes are also valuable nutritionally because they are low in fat and calories and provide a good source of vitamin A, as well as a useful source of vitamin C and folic acid.

ZUCCHINI

Zucchini—or, as they are known in Great Britain, courgettes—are essentially baby or young, immature fruit. If allowed to grow big, they become marrows, which are stuffed and baked in Great Britain. Zucchini range in color from pale green to dark, rich green, with plain or speckled skins and a pale, delicate flesh.

Fresh zucchini flowers are sometimes sold (usually in vegetable markets, especially in certain countries, such as Italy), but they tend to become limp and fade quickly. If you grow your own zucchini, pick the male flowers from their long stalks and cook them as soon as possible for the best results (the male flowers are more elongated, larger, and less delicate than the female flowers—the female flowers drop off as the zucchini grow in their places). Zucchini flowers are usually either stuffed or dipped in batter and deep-fried.

Choosing Zucchini

Look for zucchini that are fresh, firm, and shiny, with smooth skins. Select ones that feel heavy for their size, with no signs of blemishes or soft patches. Zucchini vary in size and length, but choose smaller zucchini if you can, because these often have the best flavor. Zucchini may be straight, curved like a banana, or slightly hook-necked in shape, depending on the variety, and small round zucchini are also available at times.

CROOKNECK SQUASH

As its name suggests, the shape of this squash has a long, curved neck, and the squash has a bulbous bottom. When young, this squash is light yellow and has slighty bumpy skin, but as it matures, it turns a deep yellow and the bumps are more pronounced. The pale meaty flesh can be eaten cooked or raw. It has a delicate flavor and can be added to soups, stews, and side dishes. This versatile vegetable can be cooked by steaming, baking, broiling, or sautéing. When choosing the squash, make sure it has firm skin without signs of shriveling.

YELLOW SQUASH

This squash is very similar to zucchini in its flavor and texture, as well as its shape, which can be either straight or have a curved neck. The main difference is that the color is yellow. Choose younger squash, which have better flavor than the mature ones.

PATTYPAN SQUASH

Also known as scalloped squash, pattypan squash is disk-shaped (like a flattened ball) with fluted or scalloped edges. It varies in color from creamy white or shades of yellow to pale or bright green. The flesh is creamy white and has a very mild flavor. Pale-green skin indicates a tender young squash—the skin becomes white as the squash matures. As with other summer squashes, the thin skin—which can be smooth or bumpy in the case of this squash—does not need to be removed for cooking. Large types are good for stuffing.

WINTER SQUASHES

Winter squashes, including pumpkins, tend to be larger and slower-growing than the summer squashes. They have hard, thicker, tough skin or rind that needs to be peeled away from the flesh (before or after cooking), leaving behind the wonderful dense, firm flesh that can then be used in so many recipes. The seeds of winter squashes are usually larger, hard, and inedible, so also need to be removed before cooking.

Preparing Winter Squashes

When peeling winter squashes, make sure you use a good, sharp knife. It can be a difficult and tedious job, but it will be well worth the effort. With some recipes, the squash or pumpkin can be cut in half or into wedges and baked, or sometimes it may be baked whole. The softened peel is then cut away after cooking or the cooked flesh is scooped out. If the squash or pumpkin needs peeling before cooking, it is a lot easier to cut it into more manageable wedges, slices, or chunks and peel them that way, instead of trying to peel it whole.

The flesh of winter squashes is usually slightly sweet, sometimes with a nutty flavor, and it tends to be darker in color than the summer squashes, ranging from yellow to deep orange—in general, the deeper the color of the flesh, the sweeter the taste will be.

Winter Squashes in Cooking

In a similar way to summer squashes, winter squashes are versatile and can be cooked in a variety of ways, either peeled, seeded, and cut into chunks, slices, or wedges, or cooked in larger sections (such as halved or in quarters) or whole, depending on the recipe. Winter squashes can be lightly steamed or boiled (then often pureed or mashed), sautéed or fried in butter or olive oil, microwaved, baked, roasted, braised, broiled, griddled, or stuffed and baked or roasted. Often the best way to enjoy and intensify the flavor of winter squashes, such as butternut squash, is to bake or roast them instead of boiling the flesh, although this will partly depend on the recipe.

Winter squashes, such as pumpkins, butternut, and buttercup squashes go well with many flavors. These include tomatoes, chiles, garlic, butter, olive oil, Parmesan cheese, cream, herbs, such as cilantro, sage, or rosemary, bacon or pancetta, red meat, such as beef or lamb, fresh and ground ginger, cinnamon, nutmeg, allspice, and orange.

Choosing Winter Squashes

Choose whole winter squashes with firm, thick, unblemished skins that are heavy for their size and show no signs of bruising or soft patches. When buying wedges, choose ones that are freshly cut, deep-colored, and moist with no signs of softening around the edges.

Storing Winter Squashes

Winter squashes, including pumpkins, need to be dried off, or "cured," in the sun to harden their skins if you want to store them successfully through the winter. They will then generally keep well for several months if they are stored correctly at a cool temperature in a frost-free place. Certain varieties, such as butternut squash, do keep well but are best eaten within a few weeks of picking. However, once the flesh of any of the winter squashes has been cut into, it will deteriorate, so it should be used as soon as possible, or stored (first remove the seeds and fiber), wrapped in plastic wrap, in the refrigerator.

Key Nutrients

Winter squashes, such as acorn and butternut, are low in fat and calories and provide a useful source of fiber and potassium and an excellent source of vitamin A (especially butternut squash). Butternut squash also provides a useful source of vitamin E.

PUMPKINS

Pumpkins (of which there are many varieties) can grow to an enormous size and, as well as being perfect for making lanterns for Halloween, they are ideal for many popular recipes, including pumpkin soup and pumpkin pie. Pumpkin flesh, once cooked, has a fine delicate, fairly sweet flavor and it produces a velvety, smooth puree, making it ideal for soups and sauces. It also makes an ideal filling for stuffed fresh pasta. Cubes of pumpkin flesh can be sautéed, steamed, or roasted and may be used in other dishes, such as risotto, bread, and biscuits. Pumpkin flesh may also be used to help thicken meat or vegetable stews (instead of using flour or cornstarch as the thickener), and cooked pumpkin puree can be frozen successfully, too. Large hollowed-out pumpkins can be used as a serving container for recipes, such as pumpkin soup. Cans of pumpkin puree are also available and can be used in some recipes in place of pureed or mashed fresh pumpkin flesh.

Choosing Pumpkins

Pumpkins vary a great deal in size and weight. When choosing pumpkins, select a firm specimen with no visible signs of bruising or soft patches and one that has ripened evenly and is fully mature. Generally speaking, the larger the pumpkin, the less flavor the flesh will have, so for a Halloween face lantern the larger the better, but if you are going to eat the flesh, choose a smaller specimen to enjoy its maximum flavor. The darker the flesh, the more flavor the pumpkin will have.

Key Nutrients

Pumpkin flesh is low in calories and fat and provides a good source of vitamin A and a useful source of vitamin E.

PUMPKIN SEEDS

Oil-rich dried pumpkin seeds, either roasted or toasted, can be used in both savory and sweet dishes. They are delicious sprinkled on salads or eaten simply as a nutritious snack.

OTHER POPULAR WINTER SQUASHES

Acorn Squash: Dark green (changes to orange during storage), ribbed, and pointed in shape, like a large acorn, with pale orange or yellow flesh and a mild, slightly sweetish flavor.

Buttercup Squash: Round squash with a ring around its "flower" end; the skin is dark green with thin gray stripes. The creamy orange flesh has a sweet, nutty flavor.

Butternut Squash: Bulbous and pear-shaped squash with straw or buff-colored skin and orange flesh with a fairly sweet flavor.

Delicata Squash: Oblong-shaped creamy squash with green stripes, its golden flesh tastes somewhat like sweet potato.

Hubbard Squash: Large, squash with warty skin (the skin may also be ridged), green when unripe and orange when mature (can be eaten unripe or mature). Skin color varies from green to bluish green-gray to orange (or red). The flesh is pale orange.

Kabocha Squash: A large pumpkin-shaped squash that ranges in color from dark green to bright orange. Its sweet, rich flesh is similar to that of a potato when cooked.

Red Kuri Squash: Big, teardrop-shaped squash, with deep orange skin and flesh.

Spaghetti Squash: Stubby or oval-shaped squash with bright, rich yellow, golden, or pale creamy white skin, whose flesh separates into a mass of tangled, spaghetti-like threads or strands when it is cooked. Flesh has a sweet and fresh flavor. Spaghetti squash is usually either boiled or baked whole—break the stem off, then pierce that end deeply to prevent the squash from bursting during cooking (and to let the heat penetrate the inside of the squash), then boil or bake for about 40 minutes, or until the flesh is tender (or cut in half and steam until tender). The cooked squash is then cut in half lengthwise and the flesh is scooped or "combed" out of the shell with a fork. Cooked spaghetti squash is usually served with butter, perhaps a little grated cheese and freshly ground black pepper, or tossed with a simple tomato or meat-based sauce. The cooled, cooked strands may also be used to make a salad, tossed with other salad vegetables and a simple vinaigrette.

the perfect
start

pumpkin soup

SERVES 4

- 2 tbsp olive oil
- 1 onion, chopped
- 1 garlic clove, chopped
- 1 tbsp chopped fresh ginger
- 1 small red chile, seeded and finely chopped
- 2 tbsp chopped fresh cilantro
- 1 bay leaf
- 2 lb 4 oz/1 kg pumpkin, peeled, seeded, and diced
- $2^1/_2$ cups vegetable stock
- salt and pepper
- light cream, to garnish

1 Heat the oil in a pan over medium heat. Add the onion and garlic and cook, stirring, for about 4 minutes, until slightly softened. Add the ginger, chile, cilantro, bay leaf, and pumpkin, and cook for another 3 minutes.

2 Pour in the stock and bring to a boil. Using a slotted spoon, skim any foam from the surface. Reduce the heat and simmer gently, stirring occasionally, for about 25 minutes, or until the pumpkin is tender. Remove from the heat, take out the bay leaf, and let cool a little.

3 Transfer the soup into a food processor or blender and process until smooth (you may have to do this in batches). Return the mixture to the rinsed-out pan and season to taste with salt and pepper. Reheat gently, stirring. Remove from the heat, pour into warmed soup bowls, garnish each one with a swirl of cream, and serve.

kidney bean, pumpkin & tomato soup

SERVES 4–6

- 9 oz/250 g dried kidney beans
- 1 tbsp olive oil
- 2 onions, finely chopped
- 4 garlic cloves, finely chopped
- 1 celery stalk, thinly sliced
- 1 carrot, halved and thinly sliced
- 5 cups water
- 2 tsp tomato paste
- $\frac{1}{8}$ tsp dried thyme
- $\frac{1}{8}$ tsp dried oregano
- $\frac{1}{8}$ tsp ground cumin
- 1 bay leaf
- 14 oz/400 g canned chopped tomatoes
- 9 oz/250 g peeled pumpkin flesh, diced
- $\frac{1}{4}$ tsp chili paste, or to taste
- salt and pepper
- fresh cilantro, to garnish

1 Pick over the beans, cover generously with cold water, and let soak for 6 hours, or overnight. Drain the beans, put in a saucepan, and add enough cold water to cover by 2 inches/5 cm. Bring to a boil and simmer for 10 minutes. Drain and rinse well.

2 Heat the oil in a large saucepan over medium heat. Add the onions, cover, and cook for 3–4 minutes, until they are just softened, stirring occasionally. Add the garlic, celery, and carrot, and continue cooking for 2 minutes.

3 Add the water, drained beans, tomato paste, thyme, oregano, cumin, and bay leaf. When the mixture begins to bubble, reduce the heat to low. Cover and simmer gently for 1 hour, stirring occasionally.

4 Stir in the tomatoes, pumpkin, and chili paste and continue simmering for an additional hour, or until the beans and pumpkin are tender, stirring from time to time.

5 Season to taste with salt and pepper and stir in a little more chili paste, if desired. Ladle the soup into bowls, garnish with cilantro, and serve.

roasted squash, sweet potato & garlic soup

SERVES 6–8

- 1 sweet potato, about 12 oz/350 g
- 1 acorn squash
- 4 shallots, peeled
- 2 tbsp olive oil
- 5–6 garlic cloves, unpeeled
- 3³/₄ cups chicken stock
- ¹/₂ cup light cream
- salt and pepper
- snipped chives, to garnish

1 Preheat the oven to 375°F/190°C.

2 Cut the sweet potato, squash, and shallots in half lengthwise, through to the stem end. Scoop the seeds out of the squash. Brush the cut sides with the oil.

3 Put the vegetables, cut-side down, in a shallow roasting pan. Add the garlic cloves. Roast in the preheated oven for about 40 minutes, until tender and light brown.

4 When cool, scoop the flesh from the potato and squash halves, and put in a saucepan with the shallots. Remove the garlic peel and add the soft insides to the other vegetables.

5 Add the stock and a pinch of salt. Bring just to a boil, reduce the heat, and simmer, partially covered, for about 30 minutes, stirring occasionally, until the vegetables are very tender.

6 Let the soup cool slightly, then transfer to a food processor or blender and process until smooth, working in batches, if necessary. (If using a food processor, strain off the cooking liquid and reserve. Process the soup solids with enough cooking liquid to moisten them, then combine with the remaining liquid.)

7 Return the soup to the rinsed-out pan and stir in the cream. Season to taste with salt and pepper, then simmer for 5–10 minutes, until completely heated through. Ladle into warmed serving bowls, garnish with pepper and snipped chives, and serve.

curried zucchini soup

SERVES 4

- 2 tsp butter
- 1 large onion, finely chopped
- 2 lb/900 g zucchini, sliced
- 2 cups chicken or vegetable stock
- 1 tsp curry powder
- $1/2$ cup sour cream, plus extra to garnish
- salt and pepper

1 Melt the butter in a large saucepan over medium heat. Add the onion and cook for about 3 minutes, until it begins to soften.

2 Add the zucchini, stock, and curry powder, along with a large pinch of salt, if using unsalted stock. Bring the soup to a boil, reduce the heat, cover, and cook gently for about 25 minutes, until the vegetables are tender.

3 Let the soup cool slightly, then transfer to a food processor or blender, working in batches if necessary. Process the soup until just smooth, but still with green flecks. (If using a food processor, strain off the cooking liquid and reserve. Process the soup solids with enough cooking liquid to moisten them, then combine with the remaining liquid.)

4 Return the soup to the rinsed-out saucepan and stir in the sour cream. Reheat gently over a low heat just until hot. (Do not boil.)

5 Taste and adjust the seasoning, if needed. Ladle into warmed bowls, garnish with a swirl of sour cream, and serve.

butternut squash & leek soup

SERVES 4–6

- 2 tbsp olive oil
- 1 red or white onion, chopped
- 3 leeks, washed and thinly sliced (about 8 oz/225 g prepared weight)
- 2 tsp ground cumin
- 2 tsp ground coriander
- 3¹/₂ cups diced butternut squash
- 5 cups vegetable stock
- salt and pepper
- chopped fresh cilantro or parsley, to garnish

1 Heat the olive oil in a large pan, add the onion and leeks, and sauté for about 5 minutes, until softened. Add the ground spices and cook gently for 1 minute, stirring. Stir in the squash, stock, and seasoning. Cover, bring to a boil, then reduce the heat, and simmer for about 25 minutes, until the vegetables are tender, stirring occasionally.

2 Remove the pan from the heat and cool slightly, then process the soup using a handheld mixer (or in a blender or food processor) until smooth and combined. Gently reheat the soup until hot, stirring. Ladle into warm soup bowls, garnish with a sprinkling of chopped herbs, and serve with fresh crusty bread.

mini butternut squash pancakes with plum tomatoes & parma ham

SERVES 4

pancakes
- 4¾ oz/130 g, peeled weight, butternut squash
- generous ¼ cup low-fat plain yogurt
- 1 tsp maple syrup
- pinch of cayenne pepper
- 1 tsp canola or vegetable oil, plus extra for oiling the pan
- pinch of baking powder
- 4 tsp whole wheat flour
- 1 medium egg white, lightly beaten

filling
- 10½ oz/300 g baby plum tomatoes
- 2 tbsp balsamic vinegar
- 1 tsp maple syrup
- 1 tsp finely chopped fresh thyme
- 4 thin slices Parma ham, all visible fat removed

1 Preheat the oven to 350°F/180°C.

2 To make the pancakes, halve the peeled butternut squash and scoop out the seeds. Cut the flesh into chunks and spread out on a nonstick baking sheet. Roast for 15–20 minutes, or until tender but not colored.

3 Using a handheld electric mixer, blend the squash with the yogurt, maple syrup, cayenne, oil and baking powder in a large bowl until smooth, or use a food processor. Beat in the flour, then fold in the egg white.

4 Spray a nonstick skillet lightly with oil and heat until just smoking. Pour in a level tablespoonful of the batter and cook until bubbles appear on the surface. Flip over and cook for an additional 1–2 minutes. Remove and keep warm. Repeat with the remaining batter. You will need 3 pancakes per serving.

5 Meanwhile, preheat the broiler to hot. Halve the tomatoes, place in a large bowl with the vinegar, maple syrup, and thyme and gently mix. Transfer to a nonstick baking sheet and broil for 4 minutes. Add the Parma ham to the edges of the sheet and broil for 2 minutes, or until crispy.

6 To serve, layer the pancakes with the tomatoes and top with the Parma ham. Drizzle over the cooking juices and serve.

summer zucchini
ribbon salad

SERVES 4–6

dressing
- 4 tbsp extra virgin olive oil
- 1 tbsp freshly squeezed lemon juice or white wine vinegar
- $\frac{1}{2}$–1 tsp Dijon mustard
- pinch of superfine sugar
- 1 small garlic clove, crushed (optional)
- salt and pepper

salad
- 2 green zucchini (about 10 oz/280 g total weight)
- 2 yellow zucchini (about 10 oz/280 g total weight)
- 1 large carrot (about 7 oz/ 200 g)
- 4 oz/115 g French breakfast radishes, thinly sliced
- 4–6 scallions, chopped
- 2–3 tbsp shredded fresh basil leaves
- Parmesan cheese shavings, to garnish (optional)

1   Make the dressing. Put the olive oil, lemon juice, mustard, sugar, garlic, if using, and seasoning in a small bowl and whisk together until thoroughly mixed. Set aside. Make the salad. Using a vegetable peeler, cut the green and yellow zucchini into long, thin ribbons, avoiding the seeds in the center (discard the cores).

2   Put into a salad bowl. Repeat with the carrot to make long, thin ribbons, then add these to the zucchini ribbons, together with the radishes, scallions, and shredded basil. Toss gently to mix. Briefly whisk the dressing, then drizzle it over the salad and toss gently to coat. Serve immediately, garnishing each portion with a sprinkling of Parmesan shavings, if you like.

honey-glazed
sautéed squash

SERVES 4

- 3 tbsp butter
- 3 tbsp honey
- scant 4 cups diced winter squash
- 1 tsp finely chopped fresh thyme
- salt and pepper
- fresh thyme sprigs, to garnish

Put the butter and honey in a nonstick skillet and heat gently until melted. Add the squash cubes, chopped thyme, and seasoning and mix well. Sauté over medium heat for 8–10 minutes, turning and tossing frequently, until the squash cubes are tender and glazed all over (the glaze will gradually thicken and coat them). Garnish with thyme sprigs and serve as an appetizer with fresh bread, or as an accompaniment with broiled chicken, red meat, or fish.

red bell pepper &
zucchini stacks

SERVES 6

- 2 tsp olive oil
- 1 small red bell pepper, seeded and finely chopped
- generous $^3/_4$ cup finely chopped zucchini
- 1 garlic clove, crushed
- scant $^1/_4$ cup finely chopped sun-dried tomatoes in oil, patted dry
- 1–2 tbsp finely shredded fresh basil leaves, plus extra to garnish
- 4 tbsp prepared smooth tomato salsa or classic green pesto
- 18 chilled fresh small/mini (cocktail) blinis ($2^1/_4$–$2^1/_2$ inches/ 5.5–6 cm in diameter each)
- $^1/_2$ cup grated mozzarella or cheddar cheese
- $^1/_4$ cup finely grated Parmesan cheese
- 5 tbsp thick sour cream or crème fraîche
- salt and pepper

1 Preheat the oven to 350°F/180°C. Lightly grease a cookie sheet and set aside. Heat the olive oil in a small pan over medium-high heat. Add the bell pepper, zucchini, and garlic and sauté for 4–5 minutes.

2 Remove from the heat and stir in the sun-dried tomatoes, shredded basil, and seasoning, mixing well. Set aside. Spread $^1/_2$ teaspoon of salsa on one side of each blini. To assemble the stacks, place one blini, coated-side up, on a cutting board. Spoon a little (about 1 heaping tablespoon) of the sautéed vegetable mixture on top of the blini and level the surface. Sprinkle a little mozzarella cheese over the vegetables. Place a second blini on top, coated-side up, top with a spoonful of the vegetable mixture, and level the surface, then sprinkle with mozzarella. Place a third blini on top, coated-side up. Place the blini stack on the prepared cookie sheet.

3 Repeat this procedure with the remaining blinis, sautéed vegetables, and mozzarella to make a total of 6 blinis stacks. Sprinkle the Parmesan cheese evenly over the top of the blinis stacks. Bake for 8–10 minutes, until the blinis are hot and the cheese is melting. Meanwhile, combine the sour cream and the remaining salsa in a small bowl. Garnish the cooked blinis stacks with a sprinkling of shredded basil and serve immediately with a spoonful of salsa -flavored sour cream on top or on the side.

simple & light

couscous salad with roasted butternut squash

SERVES 4

- 2 tbsp honey
- 4 tbsp olive oil
- 1 butternut squash, peeled, seeded, and cut into ³/₄-inch/2-cm chunks
- heaping 1¼ cups couscous
- 1¾ cups low-salt vegetable stock
- ½ cucumber, diced
- 1 zucchini, diced
- 1 red bell pepper, seeded and diced
- juice of ½ lemon
- salt and pepper
- 2 tbsp chopped fresh parsley, to garnish

1 Preheat the oven to 375°F/190°C. Mix half the honey with 1 tablespoon of the oil in a large bowl, add the squash, and toss well to coat. Tip into a roasting pan and roast in the preheated oven for 30–40 minutes, until soft and golden.

2 Meanwhile, put the couscous in a heatproof bowl. Heat the stock in a pan and pour over the couscous, cover, and let stand for 3 minutes. Add 1 tablespoon of the remaining oil and fork through, then stir in the diced cucumber, zucchini, and red bell pepper. Re-cover and keep warm.

3 Whisk the remaining honey and oil with the lemon juice in a pitcher and season to taste with salt and pepper. Stir the mixture through the couscous.

4 To serve, top the couscous with the roasted squash and sprinkle with the parsley.

roasted butternut
squash

SERVES 4

- 1 butternut squash, about 1 lb/450 g
- 1 onion, chopped
- 2–3 garlic cloves, crushed
- 4 small tomatoes, chopped
- 3 oz/85 g cremini mushrooms, chopped
- 3 oz/85 g canned lima beans, drained, rinsed, and coarsely chopped
- 1 zucchini, about 4 oz/115 g, trimmed and grated
- 1 tbsp chopped fresh oregano, plus extra to garnish
- 2 tbsp tomato paste
- 1¼ cups water
- 4 scallions, trimmed and chopped
- 1 tbsp Worcestershire or hot pepper sauce, or to taste
- pepper

1 Preheat the oven to 375°F/190°C. Prick the squash all over with a metal skewer, then roast for 40 minutes, or until tender. Remove from the oven and let stand until cool enough to handle.

2 Cut the squash in half, scoop out and discard the seeds, then scoop out some of the flesh, making hollows in both halves. Chop the scooped-out flesh and put in a bowl. Place the two halves side by side in a large roasting pan.

3 Add the onion, garlic, chopped tomatoes, and mushrooms to the cooked squash flesh. Add the coarsely chopped lima beans, grated zucchini, chopped oregano, and pepper to taste and mix well. Spoon the filling into the 2 halves of the squash, packing it down as firmly as possible.

4 Mix the tomato paste with the water, scallions, and Worcestershire sauce in a small bowl and pour around the squash.

5 Cover loosely with a large sheet of foil and bake for 30 minutes, or until piping hot. Serve, divided equally among 4 warmed bowls, garnished with extra chopped oregano.

butternut
squash stir-fry

SERVES 4

- 2 lb/900 g butternut squash, peeled
- 3 tbsp peanut oil
- 1 onion, sliced
- 2 garlic cloves, crushed
- 1 tsp coriander seeds
- 1 tsp cumin seeds
- 2 tbsp chopped fresh cilantro
- generous ⅓ cup coconut milk
- ½ cup water
- ⅔ cup salted cashews

garnish
- freshly grated lime rind
- fresh cilantro
- lime wedges

1　Slice the butternut squash into small, bite-size cubes, using a sharp knife.

2　Heat the peanut oil in a large preheated wok.

3　Add the butternut squash, onion, and garlic and cook for 5 minutes.

4　Stir in the coriander seeds, cumin seeds, and fresh cilantro and cook for 1 minute.

5　Add the coconut milk and water to the wok and bring to a boil. Cover the wok and simmer for 10–15 minutes, or until the squash is tender.

6　Add the cashews and stir to combine.

7　Transfer the stir-fry to warm serving dishes and garnish with freshly grated lime zest, fresh cilantro, and lime wedges. Serve hot.

stuffed pumpkin
with gruyère cheese

SERVES 4

- 1 large pumpkin
- 1¼ cups heavy cream
- 3 garlic cloves, thinly sliced
- 1 tbsp fresh thyme leaves
- 4½ oz/125 g grated Gruyère cheese
- salt and pepper
- crusty bread
- watercress, arugula, or spinach salad, to serve

1 Preheat the oven to 350°F/180°C.

2 Cut horizontally straight through the top quarter of the pumpkin to form a lid. Scoop out the seeds. Put the pumpkin in a large, deep ovenproof dish. Heat the cream and garlic together in a saucepan until just below boiling point. Remove from the heat, then season to taste with salt and pepper and stir in the thyme. Pour into the pumpkin and pop the lid on top.

3 Bake in the preheated oven for 1 hour, or until the flesh is tender—the exact cooking time will depend on the size of the pumpkin. Be careful to avoid overcooking the pumpkin, or it may collapse. Remove from the oven, then lift off the lid and scatter over the Gruyère cheese. Return to the oven and bake for an additional 10 minutes.

4 Serve the soft pumpkin flesh with a generous portion of the cheesy cream, some good crusty bread, and a salad of peppery watercress, arugula, or spinach leaves.

chargrilled pumpkin wedges with goat cheese & prosciutto

SERVES 4

- 10½ oz/300 g pumpkin flesh (peeled and seeded weight), cut into thin wedges or slices
- 1 red or yellow bell pepper, seeded and sliced into strips
- 1 small red onion, thinly sliced
- 3 tbsp olive oil
- 1 tbsp freshly squeezed lemon juice
- 1 tsp Dijon mustard
- 3½-oz/100-g goat cheese log (with rind), cut into 8 thin or 4 medium slices
- 4 thin slices prosciutto
- salt and pepper
- chopped fresh parsley, to garnish

1 Preheat the broiler to medium-high. Line the rack in a large broiler pan with foil and set aside. Place the pumpkin, bell pepper, and onion in a large bowl. In a separate small bowl, whisk together the olive oil, lemon juice, mustard, and seasoning until combined.

2 Pour the oil mixture over the vegetables and toss gently to coat. Spread the vegetables in a single layer on the prepared broiler rack and broil for 10–15 minutes, until the vegetables are tender and cooked to your liking, turning halfway through cooking.

3 Divide the broiled vegetables among 4 warm heatproof serving plates and drizzle any juices over them. Top each portion with 1 or 2 slices (depending on the thickness of the slices) of goat cheese and broil briefly until the cheese just begins to melt. Top each portion with a slice of prosciutto and sprinkle with chopped parsley. Serve immediately with fresh crusty bread.

pumpkin soufflé

SERVES 4–6

- 2²/₃ cups diced pumpkin
- 2 tbsp butter, diced, plus extra for greasing
- 2 tbsp finely grated Parmesan cheese
- ¹/₄ cup all-purpose flour
- generous 1 cup milk
- 4 eggs, separated, plus 1 extra egg white
- 1 cup finely grated sharp cheddar cheese
- 1 tsp Dijon mustard
- salt and pepper
- cooked fresh vegetables, to serve

1 Cook the pumpkin in a pan of boiling water for about 10 minutes, until tender. Drain well, then mash the flesh and set aside. Preheat the oven to 375°F/190°C. Grease a 2³/₄-quart/2¹/₂-liter, 8-inch/20-cm soufflé dish with butter, then sprinkle with the Parmesan, coating the bottom and sides evenly. Set aside. Put the diced butter, flour, and milk in a pan and heat gently, whisking constantly, until the sauce comes to a boil and thickens. Simmer for 3 minutes, stirring.

2 Transfer the sauce to a large bowl, add the mashed pumpkin, and mix well. Gradually beat in the egg yolks and all but 2 tablespoons of the cheddar cheese, then stir in the mustard, and season with salt and pepper. Place a cookie sheet in the oven to preheat. Whisk the egg whites in a separate, clean, dry bowl until stiff (this is easiest to do with an electric handheld mixer), then carefully fold them into the pumpkin mixture.

3 Pour the mixture gently into the prepared dish and sprinkle with the remaining cheddar. Stand the dish on the cookie sheet in the oven and bake for 25–30 minutes, until well risen, golden brown, and lightly set (just firm to the touch). Serve immediately with cooked fresh vegetables, such as green beans and broccoli florets.

thai-spiced chicken
with zucchini

SERVES 4

- 1 tbsp olive oil
- 1 garlic clove, finely chopped
- 1-inch/2.5-cm piece fresh ginger, finely chopped
- 1 small fresh red chile, seeded and finely chopped
- 12 oz/350 g skinless, boneless chicken breast portions, cut into thin strips
- 1 tbsp Thai 7-spice seasoning
- 1 red bell pepper and 1 bell yellow pepper, seeded and sliced
- 2 zucchini, thinly sliced
- 8 oz/225 g canned bamboo shoots, drained
- 2 tbsp dry sherry or apple juice
- 1 tbsp light soy sauce
- 2 tbsp chopped fresh cilantro, plus extra to garnish
- salt and pepper
- cooked rice or egg noodles, to serve

1 Heat the olive oil in a nonstick wok or large skillet. Add the garlic, ginger, and chile and stir-fry for 30 seconds to release the flavors. Add the chicken and Thai seasoning and stir-fry for 4 minutes, until the chicken has colored all over.

2 Add the bell peppers and zucchini and stir-fry for 1–2 minutes, until slightly softened. Stir in the bamboo shoots and stir-fry for an additional 2–3 minutes, until the chicken is cooked through and tender.

3 Add the sherry or apple juice, soy sauce, and seasoning and sizzle for 1–2 minutes. Stir in the chopped cilantro and serve immediately garnished with extra cilantro. Serve with cooked rice or egg noodles.

zucchini flower
fritters

SERVES 4–6

- ⅔ cup self-rising flour
- 1 tsp baking powder
- 1 tbsp extra virgin olive oil
- 1 egg, beaten
- generous ¾–1 cup iced water
- olive oil, for frying
- 16–20 zucchini blossoms
- salt and pepper
- sea salt flakes
- lemon wedges, for serving

1 Sift the flour and baking powder together into a bowl and add the extra virgin olive oil and egg. Stir in enough of the water to make a batter with the consistency of heavy cream (the exact quantity may vary according to the flour used). Season to taste with salt and a little pepper.

2 Pour a shallow layer of olive oil into a large skillet or wok and heat over high heat until very hot. Dip the zucchini blossoms briefly in the batter, then add to the oil and cook, in batches, for 2–4 minutes, or until crisp and golden. Remove with a slotted spoon and drain on paper towels. Serve immediately, lightly sprinkled with sea salt flakes and with lemon wedges for squeezing over.

zucchini, carrot & tomato frittata

SERVES 4

- 2 sprays olive oil
- 1 onion, cut into small wedges
- 1–2 garlic cloves, crushed
- 2 eggs
- 2 egg whites
- 1 zucchini, about 3 oz/85 g, trimmed and grated
- 2 carrots, about 4 oz/115 g, peeled and grated
- 2 tomatoes, chopped
- pepper
- 1 tbsp shredded fresh basil, for sprinkling

1 Heat the oil in a large nonstick skillet, add the onion and garlic, and sauté for 5 minutes, stirring frequently. Beat the eggs and egg whites together in a bowl then pour into the skillet. Using a spatula or fork, pull the egg mixture from the sides of the skillet into the center.

2 Once the bottom has set lightly, add the grated zucchini and carrots with the tomatoes. Add pepper to taste and continue to cook over low heat until the eggs are set to personal preference.

3 Sprinkle with the shredded basil, cut the frittata into quarters, and serve.

griddled zucchini
bruschetta

SERVES 4

- 1 tbsp olive oil, plus extra for drizzling
- ½ tsp ground cumin
- 2 zucchini (about 10½ oz/ 300 g total weight), halved crosswise, then thinly sliced lengthwise
- 1 red onion, thinly sliced
- 2 large plum tomatoes or vine-ripened tomatoes, thickly sliced (each cut into 4 slices)
- 8 slices (each about ¾ inch/ 2 cm thick) plain ciabatta bread (or 8 slices cut from a large French baguette or white flute)
- 1 garlic clove, halved
- salt and pepper
- shredded fresh basil leaves, to garnish
- thin Parmesan cheese shavings, to serve (optional)

1 In a large bowl, whisk together the olive oil, cumin, and seasoning. Add the zucchini and onion slices and toss gently to coat all over. Heat a nonstick ridged grill pan over medium heat. Place a layer of zucchini and onion slices on the pan and cook for 6–8 minutes, until lightly browned and tender, turning occasionally. When the first batch is cooked, remove and keep warm, then add the remaining zucchini and onion slices to the grill pan, and cook as before.

2 Remove and keep warm. Add the tomato slices to the grill pan and cook briefly on both sides (about 1 minute on each side), then remove and keep warm. Carefully wipe out any stray tomato seeds from the pan using paper towels, if necessary. Add the bread slices to the grill pan and toast each side, turning once. Remove from the pan to warmed serving plates. Rub the toasts on one side with the cut garlic halves, then drizzle with a little olive oil. Arrange the grilled vegetables on top of the garlicky toasts and sprinkle with Parmesan shavings, if you like. Sprinkle with shredded basil and serve immediately.

hearty & warming

chicken, pumpkin & chorizo casserole

SERVES 4

- 3 tbsp olive oil
- 5 lb/2.25 kg chicken, cut into 8 pieces and dusted with flour
- 7 oz/200 g fresh chorizo sausages, thickly sliced
- a small bunch of fresh sage leaves
- 1 onion, chopped
- 6 garlic cloves, sliced
- 2 celery stalks, sliced
- 1 small pumpkin or butternut squash, peeled and roughly chopped
- 1 cup dry sherry
- 2$^{1}/_{2}$ cups chicken stock
- 14 oz/400 g canned chopped tomatoes
- 2 bay leaves
- salt and pepper
- 1 tbsp chopped fresh flat-leaf parsley, to garnish

1 Preheat the oven to 350°F/180°C.

2 Heat the oil in a casserole dish and fry the chicken with the chorizo and sage leaves, until golden brown. Remove with a slotted spoon and reserve. You may need to do this in two batches.

3 Add the onion, garlic, celery, and pumpkin and cook until the mixture begins to brown slightly.

4 Add the sherry, chicken stock, tomatoes, and bay leaves, and season with salt and pepper to taste.

5 Return the reserved chicken, chorizo, and sage to the casserole, cover, and cook in the oven for 1 hour.

6 Remove the casserole from the oven, uncover, stir in the chopped parsley and serve.

green pumpkin curry

SERVES 4

- ²/₃ cup vegetable oil
- 2 medium onions, sliced
- ¹/₂ tsp white cumin seeds
- scant 4 cups chopped green pumpkin
- 1 tsp dried mango powder
- 1 tsp finely chopped fresh ginger
- 1 tsp crushed garlic
- 1 tsp crushed dried red chile
- ¹/₂ tsp salt
- 1¹/₄ cups water
- chapatis or naan bread, to serve

1 Heat the vegetable oil in a large heavy skillet. Add the onions and cumin seeds and fry over medium heat, stirring occasionally, for about 5 minutes, until the onions are softened and a light golden brown and the seeds are giving off their aroma.

2 Add the cubed pumpkin to the skillet and stir-fry over low heat for 3–5 minutes.

3 Combine the dried mango powder, ginger, garlic, chile, and salt. Add the spice mixture to the pan, stirring well to combine with the vegetables.

4 Add the water, cover, and cook over low heat, stirring occasionally, for 10–15 minutes.

5 Transfer to serving plates and serve with chapatis or naan bread.

penne with pumpkin sauce

SERVES 4

- 4 tbsp unsalted butter
- 4 oz/115 g white onions or shallots, very finely chopped
- 1 lb 12 oz/800 g pumpkin, unprepared weight
- pinch of freshly grated nutmeg
- 12 oz/350 g dried penne or radiatore
- generous ¾ cup light cream
- 4 tbsp freshly grated Parmesan cheese, plus extra to serve
- 2 tbsp chopped fresh flat-leaf parsley
- salt and pepper

1 Melt the butter in a heavy-bottom saucepan over low heat. Add the onions, sprinkle with a little salt, cover, and cook, stirring frequently, for 25–30 minutes.

2 Scoop out and discard the seeds from the pumpkin. Peel and finely chop the flesh. Put the pumpkin into the saucepan and season to taste with nutmeg. Cover and cook over low heat, stirring occasionally, for 45 minutes.

3 Meanwhile, bring a large saucepan of lightly salted water to a boil. Add the pasta, return to a boil, and cook for 8–10 minutes, or until tender but still firm to the bite. Drain thoroughly, reserving about ⅔ cup of the cooking liquid.

4 Stir the cream, grated Parmesan cheese, and parsley into the pumpkin sauce and season to taste with salt and pepper. If the mixture seems a little too thick, add some or all of the reserved cooking liquid and stir. Put in the pasta and toss for 1 minute. Serve immediately, with extra Parmesan cheese for sprinkling.

root vegetable & pumpkin casserole

SERVES 4–6

- 1 onion, sliced
- 2 leeks, sliced
- 2 celery stalks, chopped
- 2 carrots, thinly sliced
- 1 red bell pepper, seeded and sliced
- 1^3/$_4$ cups diced pumpkin
- 1^2/$_3$ cups diced mixed root vegetables, such as sweet potato, parsnip, and rutabaga
- 14 oz/400 g canned chopped tomatoes
- ^{2}/$_3$–1 cup hard cider
- 2 tsp dried herbes de Provence
- salt and pepper
- chopped fresh herbs, to garnish

1 Preheat the oven to 350°F/180°C. Put the onion, leeks, celery, carrots, bell pepper, pumpkin, and root vegetables in a large casserole and mix well. Stir in the tomatoes, ^{2}/$_3$ cup of the hard cider, the dried herbs, and seasoning, mixing well.

2 Cover and bake in the center of the oven for 1^1/$_4$–1^1/$_2$ hours, until the vegetables are cooked through and tender, stirring once or twice and adding a little extra hard cider, if necessary. Garnish with a sprinkling of chopped fresh herbs and serve with warm crusty bread.

spinach & butternut squash bake

SERVES 2

- 9 oz/250 g peeled weight, butternut squash, seeded and cut into bite-size cubes
- 2 small red onions, each cut into 8 segments
- 2 tsp vegetable oil
- 4¼ oz/120 g baby spinach leaves
- 2 tbsp whole wheat breadcrumbs
- pepper

white sauce
- generous 1 cup skim milk
- heaping 2 tbsp all-purpose flour
- 1 tsp mustard powder
- 1 small onion
- 2 small bay leaves
- 4 tsp grated Parmesan or pecorino cheese

1 Preheat the oven to 400°F/200°C and warm an ovenproof serving dish.

2 Arrange the prepared squash and onion on a nonstick baking sheet and coat with the oil and plenty of black pepper. Bake for 20 minutes, turning once.

3 To make the sauce, put the milk into a small nonstick saucepan with the flour, mustard, onion, and bay leaves. Whisk over a medium heat until thick. Remove from the heat, discard the onion and bay leaves, and stir in the cheese. Set aside, stirring occasionally, to prevent a skin from forming.

4 When the squash is nearly cooked, put the spinach in a large skillet with 1 tablespoon of water, stirring, for 2–3 minutes, or until just wilted.

5 You can continue cooking this dish in the hot oven, or preheat the broiler to medium-high. Put half the squash mixture in the warmed ovenproof dish and top with half the spinach. Repeat the layers. Pour over the white sauce and sprinkle over the breadcrumbs.

6 Either put under the preheated broiler until browned and bubbling, or transfer to the oven for 15–20 minutes.

pasta with spiced leek, butternut squash & cherry tomatoes

SERVES 4

- 5½ oz/150 g baby leeks, cut into ¾-inch/2-cm slices
- 5½ oz/150 g butternut squash (peeled weight), seeded and cut into ¾-inch/2-cm chunks
- 1½ tbsp prepared medium curry paste
- 1 tsp vegetable oil
- 6 oz/175 g cherry tomatoes
- 9 oz/250 g dried pasta of your choice
- 1¼ cups White Sauce (see page 64)
- 2 tbsp chopped fresh cilantro leaves

1 Preheat the oven to 400°F/200°C.

2 Bring a large saucepan of water to a boil, add the leeks, and cook for 2 minutes. Add the butternut squash and cook for an additional 2 minutes. Drain in a colander.

3 Mix the curry paste with the oil in a large bowl. Toss the leeks and butternut squash in the mixture to coat thoroughly.

4 Transfer the leeks and butternut squash to a nonstick baking sheet and roast in the oven for 10 minutes, until golden brown. Add the tomatoes and roast for an additional 5 minutes.

5 Meanwhile, cook the pasta according to the instructions on the package and drain.

6 Put the sauce into a large saucepan and warm over a low heat. Add the leeks, butternut squash, tomatoes, and cilantro and stir in the warm pasta. Mix thoroughly and serve.

roasted squash wedges with 3-grain risotto & asparagus

SERVES 4

- 7 oz/200 g acorn squash or other type of squash, peeled, seeded, and cut into 4 wedges
- 1 tsp vegetable oil
- 3½ oz/100 g onion (peeled weight), finely chopped
- 1 tsp crushed garlic
- ⅓ cup mixed-grain risotto mix (such as short-grain rice, spelt, and pearl barley)
- 2½ cups vegetable stock
- 8¼ oz/235 g asparagus tips
- 2 tbsp finely chopped fresh marjoram, plus extra to garnish
- 3 tbsp low-fat marscapone or fromage frais
- 2 tbsp finely chopped parsley
- pepper

1 Preheat the oven to 400°F/200°C. Spread out the squash wedges on a nonstick baking sheet and roast in the oven for 20 minutes, or until tender and golden brown.

2 Meanwhile, heat the oil in a medium saucepan over a high heat, add the onion and garlic and cook, stirring, until softened but not colored. Add the risotto mix and stir in half the stock. Simmer, stirring occasionally, until the stock has reduced in the pan. Pour in the remaining stock and continue to cook, stirring occasionally, until the grains are tender.

3 Cut about thee-quarters of the asparagus into 4-inch/10-cm lengths and blanch in a saucepan of boiling water for 2 minutes. Drain and keep warm. Cut the remaining asparagus into ¼-inch/5-mm slices and add to the risotto for the last 3 minutes of the cooking time.

4 Remove the risotto from the heat and stir in the marjoram, marscapone, and parsley. Season with pepper. Do not reboil.

5 To serve, lay the squash wedges on warmed serving plates, then spoon over the risotto and top with the asparagus. Garnish with marjoram.

zucchini, goat's cheese & red onion pizza

SERVES 4–6

- 14 oz/400 g canned chopped tomatoes with herbs
- 1 tbsp olive oil
- 1 small red onion, sliced
- 2 small zucchini, sliced (about 8 oz/225 g total weight)
- 2 cups all-purpose flour
- 2 tsp baking powder
- 4 tbsp butter, diced
- scant $^1/_2$ cup milk
- $^1/_2$ cup grated mozzarella cheese
- 1 large vine-ripened tomato, thinly sliced
- 3$^1/_2$ oz/100 g soft (dry) goat cheese, crumbled
- salt and pepper
- chopped fresh parsley or basil, to garnish

1 Preheat the oven to 425°F/220°C. Grease a cookie sheet and set aside. Open the can of tomatoes and pour the entire contents into a strainer set over a bowl. Set aside, stirring occasionally, until most of the juice has drained away to leave a thick tomato pulp.

2 Reserve the tomato pulp and discard the juice. Heat the olive oil in a pan, add the onion and zucchini, and cook for about 5 minutes, until softened, stirring occasionally.

3 Remove from the heat and set aside. Sift the flour and baking powder into a bowl, add a pinch of salt, then lightly rub in the butter until the mixture resembles breadcrumbs. Stir in enough milk to form a fairly soft dough. Knead lightly. Lightly roll out the dough on a lightly floured counter to form a 10-inch/25-cm circle and put it onto the prepared cookie sheet. Spread the strained tomato pulp evenly over the dough, season with salt and pepper, then sprinkle with the mozzarella. Top with the zucchini mixture.

4 Arrange the tomato slices on top, then sprinkle the goat cheese over the tomatoes. Bake for about 25 minutes, until cooked and deep golden brown around the edges. Garnish with a sprinkling of chopped herbs and serve.

baked zucchini, cherry tomato & brie pasta

SERVES 4–6

- 1 small red onion, chopped
- 3 small zucchini, sliced (about 12 oz/350 g total weight)
- 2 tbsp olive oil
- 1 lb/450 g cherry tomatoes, halved
- 4¹/₂ cups fresh (chilled) pasta shapes, such as fusilli or riccioli
- heaping 1 cup mascarpone cheese
- 3 tbsp snipped fresh chives
- 8 oz/225 g mild Brie, diced
- ¹/₂ cup finely grated cheddar cheese
- salt and pepper
- fresh chive flowers or snipped fresh chives, to garnish
- mixed salad greens, to serve

1 Preheat the oven to 375°F/190°C. Put the onion and zucchini in a large roasting pan or shallow ovenproof dish, drizzle with 1 tablespoon of the olive oil, and toss to coat. Roast in the oven for 15 minutes, stirring once or twice. Reduce the oven temperature to 350°F/180°C.

2 Add the cherry tomatoes to the pan, placing them in a single layer on top of the vegetables with cut sides up, then drizzle with the remaining oil. Roast for an additional 10 minutes, then remove from the oven, and set aside. Meanwhile, cook the pasta in a large pan of lightly salted, boiling water for 3–5 minutes, until just cooked or al dente. Drain thoroughly and return to the rinsed-out pan.

3 Add the mascarpone, snipped chives, and seasoning to the pasta and toss to mix well. Add the roasted vegetables and their juices and stir gently to mix, being careful not to break up the tomatoes too much, then gently fold in the Brie. Transfer the mixture to a lightly greased ovenproof dish. Sprinkle the cheddar evenly over the top. Bake in the oven for 15–20 minutes, until hot and bubbling. Garnish with chive flowers and serve with mixed salad greens.

cheesy zucchini & ham gratin

SERVES 4

- 16 baby zucchini (about 1 lb 2 oz/500 g total weight)
- 4 tbsp butter
- $1/3$ cup all-purpose flour
- $1^1/4$ cups milk
- 1 tsp Dijon mustard
- 1 cup grated sharp cheddar cheese
- 8 thin slices lean smoked or unsmoked cooked ham
- $3/4$ cup fresh white or whole wheat breadcrumbs
- salt and pepper
- snipped fresh chives or chopped fresh parsley, to garnish

1 Lightly grease a shallow, ovenproof dish and set aside. Cook the zucchini in a pan of boiling water for 4–5 minutes, until tender. Drain well, set aside, and keep warm. Meanwhile, melt 3 tablespoons of the butter in a separate pan, then stir in the flour, and cook gently for 1 minute, stirring.

2 Remove the pan from the heat and gradually whisk in the milk. Return to the heat and bring gently to a boil, stirring constantly, until the sauce thickens. Simmer for 2–3 minutes, stirring. Remove the pan from the heat and stir in the mustard and ¾ cup of the cheese. Season to taste with salt and pepper. Preheat the broiler to medium-high. Cut each slice of ham in half crosswise, then wrap a half slice of ham around each zucchini. Place the ham-wrapped zucchini in a single layer in the prepared dish and pour the cheese sauce evenly over the top to cover.

3 Combine the remaining cheese and the breadcrumbs and sprinkle evenly over the cheese sauce. Dot with the remaining butter, then place under the broiler for a few minutes, until lightly browned and bubbling. Garnish with snipped chives and serve.

gourmet
delights

pumpkin chestnut risotto

SERVES 4

- 4 cups vegetable stock or chicken stock
- 1 tbsp olive oil
- 3 tbsp butter
- 1 small onion, finely chopped
- 8 oz/225 g pumpkin, diced
- 8 oz/225 g chestnuts, cooked and peeled
- scant 1¼ cups risotto rice
- ⅔ cup dry white wine
- 1 tsp crumbled saffron threads (optional)
- ¾ cup Parmesan or Grana Padano cheese, freshly grated, plus extra shavings for serving
- salt and pepper

1 Bring the stock to a boil, then reduce the heat and keep simmering gently over low heat while you are cooking the risotto.

2 Heat the oil with 2 tablespoons of the butter in a deep pan over medium heat until the butter has melted. Stir in the onion and pumpkin and cook, stirring occasionally, for 5 minutes, or until the onion is soft and starting to turn golden and the pumpkin begins to color. Coarsely chop the chestnuts and add to the mixture. Stir thoroughly to coat.

3 Reduce the heat, add the rice, and mix to coat in oil and butter. Cook, stirring constantly, for 2–3 minutes, or until the grains are translucent. Add the wine and cook, stirring constantly, for 1 minute, until it has reduced. If using the saffron threads, dissolve them in 4 tablespoons of the hot stock and add the liquid to the rice after the wine has been absorbed. Cook, stirring constantly, until the liquid has been absorbed.

4 Gradually add the hot stock, a ladleful at a time. Stir constantly and add more liquid as the rice absorbs each addition. Increase the heat to medium so that the liquid bubbles. Cook for 20 minutes, or until all the liquid is absorbed and the rice is creamy. Season to taste.

5 Remove the risotto from the heat and add the remaining butter. Mix well, then stir in the Parmesan until it melts. Adjust the seasoning if necessary, and serve at once, garnished with Parmesan shavings.

squash, sage & gorgonzola tart

SERVES 6

pie dough
- heaping ¾ cup all-purpose flour
- pinch of salt
- 5 tbsp cold butter, cut into pieces
- cold water

filling
- ½ small butternut squash or 1 slice pumpkin, weighing 9 oz/250 g
- 1 tsp olive oil
- generous 1 cup heavy cream
- 6 oz/175 g Gorgonzola cheese
- 2 eggs, plus 1 egg yolk
- 6–8 fresh sage leaves
- salt and pepper

1 Cut the squash in half and brush the cut side with the oil. Place cut-side up on a baking sheet and bake for 30–40 minutes, until browned and very soft. Let cool. Remove the seeds and scoop out the flesh into a large bowl, discarding the skin.

2 Lightly grease a 9-inch/22-cm loose-bottom fluted tart pan. Sift the flour and salt into a food processor, add the butter, and process until the mixture resembles fine breadcrumbs. Pour the mixture into a large bowl and add a little cold water, just enough to bring the dough together. Turn out onto a floured counter and roll out the dough 3¼ inches/ 8 cm larger than the pan. Carefully lift the dough into the pan and press to fit. Roll the rolling pin over the pan to neaten the edges and remove the excess dough from the edges. Fit a piece of parchment paper into the tart shell, fill with pie weights or dried beans, and let chill in the refrigerator for 30 minutes. Meanwhile, preheat the oven to 375°F/190°C.

3 Remove the pastry shell from the refrigerator and bake the tart shell with the weights for 10 minutes in the preheated oven, then remove the weights and paper. Return to the oven for 5 minutes.

4 Mash the squash and mix with half the cream, season with salt and pepper, and spread in the pastry shell. Slice the cheese and lay it on top. Whisk the remaining cream with the eggs and egg yolk and pour the mixture into the tart pan, making sure it settles evenly. Arrange the sage leaves in a circle on the surface. Bake for 30–35 minutes and let stand for 10 minutes in the pan before serving.

orange & squash
marmalade

MAKES ABOUT 5 LB/2.25 KG

- 2 lb/900 g acorn or butternut squash (peeled and seeded weight), cut into small chunks
- 6 blood oranges, scrubbed
- $2/3$ cup freshly squeezed lemon juice
- small piece fresh ginger, peeled and grated
- 2 serrano chiles, seeded and finely sliced
- 5 cups water
- 2 lb 12 oz/1.25 kg sugar

1 Place the squash in a large pan with a tight-fitting lid. Thinly slice 2 of the oranges without peeling, reserving the seeds, and add to the pan. Peel the remaining oranges and chop the flesh, then add to the pan, together with the lemon juice, grated ginger, and sliced chiles. Tie the orange seeds up in a piece of cheesecloth and add to the pan with the water.

2 Bring to a boil. Reduce the heat, then cover and simmer gently for 1 hour, or until the squash and oranges are very soft. Remove the seeds and discard.

3 Add the sugar and heat gently, stirring, until the sugar has completely dissolved. Bring to a boil and boil rapidly for 15 minutes, or until the setting point is reached.

4 Skim if necessary, then let cool for 10 minutes. Put into warmed sterilized jars and cover the tops with wax disks. When completely cold, cover with cellophane or lids, then label and store in a cool place.

yellow zucchini
tart

SERVES 6

pie dough
- scant 1³/₄ cups all-purpose flour
- pinch of salt
- generous ¹/₂ cup cold butter, cut into pieces, plus extra for greasing
- scant ¹/₂ cup grated Parmesan cheese
- 1 egg
- cold water

filling
- 2 large yellow zucchini
- 1 tbsp salt
- generous 3 tbsp unsalted butter
- 1 bunch scallions, trimmed and finely sliced
- ²/₃ cup heavy cream
- 3 large eggs
- salt and white pepper
- 1 small bunch fresh chives, chopped

1 Grease a 10-inch/25-cm loose-bottom tart pan. Sift the flour and salt into a food processor, add the butter, and blend to combine, then put into a large bowl. Add the Parmesan cheese and mix together the egg and water. Add most of the egg mixture and work to a soft dough, using more egg mixture if needed. Turn out onto a floured counter and roll out the dough 3¹/₄-inches/8-cm larger than the pan. Carefully lift the dough into the pan and press to fit. Roll the rolling pin over the pan to neaten the edges and trim the excess dough. Fit a piece of parchment paper into the tart shell, fill with pie weights or dried beans, and let chill in the refrigerator for 30 minutes. Meanwhile, preheat the oven to 400°F/200°C.

2 Bake the tart shell with the weights for 15 minutes in the preheated oven, then remove the weights and paper and bake for an additional 5 minutes. Remove from the oven and let cool. Lower the oven temperature to 350°F/180°C.

3 Meanwhile, grate the zucchini and put in a strainer with 1 tbsp salt. Let drain for 20 minutes, then rinse and put in a clean dish towel, squeezing all the moisture from the zucchini. Keep dry.

4 Melt the butter in a wide skillet, sauté the scallions until soft, then add the zucchini and cook over medium heat for 5 minutes, until any liquid has evaporated. Let cool slightly. Whisk the cream and eggs together with the salt and pepper and chives. Spoon the zucchini into the tart shell and pour in the cream mixture, making sure it settles properly, and bake for 30 minutes. Serve hot or cold.

zucchini & parmesan bread

SERVES 10–12

- 2 cups self-rising white flour, plus extra for dusting
- 2 cups self-rising whole wheat flour or 2 cups all-purpose whole wheat flour plus 2$\frac{1}{2}$ tsp baking powder
- 1 tsp salt
- 1$\frac{1}{2}$ tsp mustard powder
- 4 tbsp butter, diced
- 1$\frac{1}{3}$ cups coarsely grated zucchini, patted dry
- 1$\frac{2}{3}$ cups finely grated Parmesan cheese
- 1 tsp finely chopped fresh thyme
- 2 eggs, beaten
- $\frac{3}{4}$ cup low-fat milk
- pepper

1 Preheat the oven to 375°F/190°C. Grease a cookie sheet and set aside. Combine the flours, salt, mustard powder, and a pinch of pepper in a large bowl, then lightly rub in the butter until the mixture resembles breadcrumbs. Stir in the zucchini, Parmesan cheese, and chopped thyme.

2 Stir in the eggs and enough milk to form a soft dough. Turn out the dough onto a lightly floured counter and knead lightly, then shape into an 8-inch/20-cm circle. Put it onto the prepared cookie sheet, then cut three fairly deep slashes in the top of the loaf using a sharp knife. Bake for 40–50 minutes, until well risen and deep golden brown. Transfer to a wire rack and let cool.

3 Serve warm or cold in slices on its own or spread with butter.

pumpkin loaf

SERVES 6

- vegetable oil, for greasing
- 1 lb/450 g pumpkin flesh
- $^1/_2$ cup butter, softened, plus extra for greasing
- $^3/_4$ cup superfine sugar
- 2 eggs, lightly beaten
- heaping 1$^1/_2$ cups all-purpose flour
- 1$^1/_2$ tsp baking powder
- $^1/_2$ tsp salt
- 1 tsp ground allspice
- 2 tbsp pumpkin seeds

1 Preheat the oven to 400°F/200°C. Grease a 9 × 5 × 3-inch/23 × 13 × 8-cm loaf pan with oil.

2 Chop the pumpkin into large pieces and wrap in buttered foil. Cook in the oven for 30–40 minutes, until they are tender. Reduce the oven temperature to 325°F/160°C. Let the pumpkin cool completely before mashing well to make a thick paste.

3 In a bowl, cream the butter and sugar together until light and fluffy. Add the beaten eggs, a little at a time. Stir in the pumpkin paste then sift in the flour, baking powder, salt, and allspice.

4 Fold the pumpkin seeds gently through the mixture in a figure-eight movement. Spoon the mixture into the prepared loaf pan. Bake in the oven for about 1$^1/_4$–1$^1/_2$ hours, or until a skewer inserted into the center of the loaf comes out clean.

5 Transfer the loaf to a cooling rack to cool, then serve, sliced and buttered, if you like.

sweet pumpkin pie

SERVES 4

- 4 lb/1.8 kg sweet pumpkin
- 1³/₄ cups sweetened condensed milk
- 2 eggs
- 1 tsp salt
- ¹/₂ tsp vanilla extract
- 1 tbsp raw sugar

pie dough
- 4 tbsp cold unsalted butter, diced, plus extra for greasing
- 1 cup all-purpose flour, plus extra for dusting
- ¹/₄ tsp baking powder
- 1¹/₂ tsp ground cinnamon
- ³/₄ tsp ground nutmeg
- ³/₄ tsp ground cloves
- ¹/₄ cup superfine sugar
- 1 egg

topping
- 2 tbsp all-purpose flour
- 4 tbsp raw sugar
- 1 tsp ground cinnamon
- 2 tbsp cold unsalted butter, diced
- heaping ²/₃ cup shelled pecans, chopped
- heaping ²/₃ cup shelled walnuts, chopped

1 Preheat the oven to 375°F/190°C. Quarter the pumpkin, remove the seeds, and set aside for roasting. Remove and discard the stem and stringy insides. Place the pumpkin quarters, face down, in a shallow roasting pan and cover with foil. Bake in the oven for 1¹/₂ hours, then remove from the oven and let cool. Scoop out the flesh and mash with a potato masher or puree it in a food processor. Drain away any excess liquid. Cover with plastic wrap and let chill until ready to use. It will keep for 3 days (or several months in a freezer).

2 To make the pie dough, first grease a 9-inch/23-cm round pie plate with butter. Sift the flour and baking powder into a large bowl. Stir in the spices and the superfine sugar. Rub in the butter with the fingertips until the mixture resembles fine breadcrumbs, then make a well in the center. Lightly beat 1 egg and pour it into the well. Mix together with a wooden spoon, then use your hands to shape the dough into a ball. Place it on a clean counter lightly dusted with flour, and roll out to a circle large enough to line the pie plate. Use it to line the plate, then trim the edge. Cover the pie plate with plastic wrap and let chill in the refrigerator for 30 minutes.

3 Preheat the oven to 425°F/220°C. To make the filling, place the pumpkin puree in a large bowl, then stir in the condensed milk and the 2 eggs. Add the salt, then stir in the vanilla extract and raw sugar. Pour into the pastry shell and bake in the oven for 15 minutes.

4 Meanwhile, make the topping. Combine the flour, sugar, and cinnamon in a bowl, rub in the butter until crumbly, then stir in the nuts. Remove the pie from the oven and reduce the heat to 350°F/180°C. Sprinkle the topping over the pie, then bake for an additional 35 minutes. Remove from the oven and serve hot or cold.

butternut squash & cinnamon tart

SERVES 6–8

pie dough
- 1¹/₂ sticks salted butter, softened
- ¹/₄ cup superfine sugar
- 1 egg yolk
- scant 2 cups all-purpose flour, sifted, plus extra for dusting

filling
- 14 oz/400 g peeled and seeded butternut squash
- ³/₄ cup packed light brown sugar
- 3 eggs, beaten
- 1 tsp ground cinnamon
- 3 tbsp dark rum
- 2 tbsp mascarpone cheese
- vanilla ice cream or cream, for serving

1 To make the pie dough, beat the butter and sugar together in a bowl until light and fluffy. Add the egg yolk and stir until fully incorporated and smooth. Gradually add the flour and mix until the dough forms a ball, being careful not to overwork the dough. Divide in half and freeze one half. Wrap the remaining dough in plastic wrap and let rest at room temperature for 20 minutes or so.

2 Roll the dough out on a floured counter and use to line a 9-inch/ 23-cm tart pan with a removable bottom. Refrigerate until required.

3 Preheat the oven to 350°F/180°C.

4 To make the filling, cut the squash into small chunks and cook in a saucepan of boiling water until tender. Drain and transfer to a food processor or blender, then whiz to a puree. Add the remaining filling ingredients and whiz again until smooth. Set the tart pan on a baking sheet and carefully fill to three-quarters full with the mixture. Transfer to the preheated oven and bake for 10–15 minutes, or until the filling is beginning to set. Pour in the remaining mixture and bake for an additional 25 minutes, or until set.

5 Remove from the oven and let cool. Serve in slices with vanilla ice cream or cream.

butternut squash & orange cake

SERVES 10–12

cake

- ³/₄ cup butter, softened, plus extra for greasing
- ³/₄ cup light brown sugar
- 3 eggs, beaten
- finely grated rind and juice of 1 orange
- 2 cups whole wheat flour
- 3 tsp baking powder
- 1 tsp ground cinnamon
- 1¹/₃ cups coarsely grated butternut squash
- generous ³/₄ cup golden raisins

topping

- 1 cup soft cheese
- ¹/₄ cup confectioner's sugar, sifted
- 1 tsp finely grated orange rind (reserved from cake ingredients)
- 2–3 tsp freshly squeezed orange juice (reserved from cake ingredients) thinly pared orange zest, to decorate

1 Preheat the oven to 350°F/180°C. Grease and line a deep 7-inch/18-cm round cake pan and set aside. For the cake, cream the butter and sugar together in a bowl until light and fluffy.

2 Gradually beat in the eggs, beating well after each addition. Reserve 1 teaspoon of the orange rind for the topping, then beat the remaining orange rind into the creamed mixture. Fold in the flour, baking powder, and cinnamon, then fold in the squash, golden raisins, and a little orange juice, if necessary (about 1 tablespoon) to create a fairly soft consistency.

3 Turn the mixture into the prepared pan and level the surface. Bake for about 1 hour, until risen, firm to the touch, and deep golden brown. Remove from the oven and cool in the pan for a few minutes, then turn out onto a wire rack. Remove the lining paper and let cool completely.

4 To make the topping, beat the soft cheese, confectioner's sugar, reserved grated orange rind, and 2–3 teaspoons of the reserved orange juice together in a bowl until smooth and combined. Spread over the top of the cold cake, swirling it attractively, then sprinkle with pared orange zest. Serve immediately in slices.